The Off-Season

The Off-Season

Jen Levitt

Four Way Books
Tribeca

for my family

Please direct all inquiries to:
Editorial Office
Four Way Books
POB 535, Village Station
New York, NY 10014
www.fourwaybooks.com

Library of Congress Cataloging-in-Publication Data

Names: Levitt, Jen author.
Title: The off-season / Jen Levitt.
Description: New York, NY : Four Way Books, 2016. | Includes bibliographical
references.
Identifiers: LCCN 2016007106 | ISBN 9781935536772 (pbk. : alk. paper)
Classification: LCC PS3612.E9345 A6 2016 | DDC 811/.6--dc23
LC record available at https://lccn.loc.gov/2016007106

This book is manufactured in the United States of America and printed on acid-free paper.

Four Way Books is a not-for-profit literary press. We are grateful for the assistance
we receive from individual donors, public arts agencies, and private foundations.

This publication is made possible with public funds from the National Endowment for the Arts

from the New York State Council on the Arts, a state agency,

and from the Jerome Foundation.

[clmp]

We are a proud member of the Community of Literary Magazines and Presses.

Distributed by University Press of New England
One Court Street, Lebanon, NH 03766

CONTENTS

4.

Foreignness Breeds That Shared Language, the Brain in Translation (Dear

Notes

1.

MODERN POEM

This is my outstretched arm.
This is the other half of my turkey sandwich.
This is a man diving into a lake, cool & deep, like magnets.
This is a picture of my mother when she was young,
wearing a winter coat & looking away from the camera.
She's holding a stick, poking the snow.
This is my red bookshelf
& the contact list on my cellular phone.
Philip Roth climbing a poem, victorious at the top.
Freud & Lacan having a picnic at the park
unable to decide whether to cut the grapes or eat them whole.
The grapes, metaphors for the unconscious.
This is the red or yellow bird from that other poem.
It makes a nest in a foreign language.
I have no idea what it is saying.
This is the teenagers on the corner with the boom boxes
who say, Wait. Take us out of the poem.
We don't even know what boom boxes are.
Okay, I say. Get out. After you turn in your homework.
This is the long sigh of the poem.
This is the pop stars on the music channels,
the hoarders, food critics & day-time talk show hosts.
The commentators on CNN speculating about a terrorist poem.
This is you & me on a conveyor belt about to board a plane.
The voice over the loudspeaker.
The terminal crowded with people trying to find their gates.

Each morning I checked the news
on gossip sites. I fried an egg,
trashed the pinkish shells.
As the kitchen filled with light
I lunged into it & waited.
At the gym a new machine turned
off when I stepped on, on the street
the same dark-haired woman,
wanting. Some days I gave a dollar,
some days I bowed my head
& walked home to watch *SVU*.
Or I got a pedicure & tensed up
when my feet were lotioned.
Water idled in a basin, then went.
I was made more valuable, like stocks.
Luckily I wasn't beautiful,
or I'd have had too many lovers
to choose from. There wouldn't have been
time to sit in my room as the snowplow
emptied, thinking about milk.

BLUE HOUSE WITH WRAP-AROUND PORCH

I am born early in the leather grip of winter

won't fall asleep for weeks then months

Before my mother's friend dies of cancer she says *I'm scared*

in the hospital room no one knows what to answer

We eat chocolate-chip pancakes & runny eggs

made by a dad row a blow-up raft down the river

in the retrograde muck where we are *becoming ourselves*

Days pass like thoughts as yet unformed

My mother's friend wears dream-catcher earrings

because they're *just so her* says *I'm scared*

& my mother: *Look at all the other*

fears you've conquered yes made it through doesn't say *alive*

On the bus route we hide under pleather seats

so the driver can't find us in his pageboy hat & sunglasses

One morning he stops the bus on a side street to pee

behind a bush takes out his thing

I think he might have been fired after that

Marriage & kids—all that unknowing

Jimmy the fifth-grade king of us arbiter of rock music

with a buzz cut & Nike high-tops: *I made my sister take*

her clothes off in front of me I saw her down there saw it good

I'm somewhere under the seats my face to the floor

I'm somewhere in another life yes this displacement starts early

My first cassette tape *Storm Front* by Billy Joel first concert

Counting Crows kiss by the concessions then not again for years

Girls of the spandex-fabric & swoop bangs

gossip about who gave hand jobs on the trip to the state capital

I talk on the phone at night before they go cordless

The blue house gets painted green I don't have a sister

In my mother's friend's kitchen washing dishes the collies must be fed who curl up under couches I sit quiet as a bed

A low moon is spreading over impossibly bright woods

I say *Show me a way out of this* I ask it in my mind

My mother's friend in Xmas photos with long hair

then no hair then gone

I AM KARL MARX

In the world there are many people
I don't know most of them
Sometimes the ones I do know say to me
You should style your hair like this
or *Why don't you get a drink from that bar over there*
I say thank you for the advice
& I may go for a drink at that bar
even though I am tired
from standing in front of teenagers all day
on a chair looking down at them
pretending to be Marx pretending they are the masses
I ask *What would I say to you, proletarians, if I were Marx?*
They say *Capitalism is tyranny! Down with the bourgeoisie!*
They are correct so I yell at them to rise up
in my best German accent
& with a white beard made of copy paper
Later I will ride home on the train
at eye-level with the gray buildings
& feeling like I sometimes do
Empiricism cannot help me
nor psychoanalysis nor meditation
It is difficult not knowing how to be in the world
which is different than not knowing
who you are, but close

DICKINSON IN PSYCHOANALYSIS

Complains of restlessness & a sharp pain

behind the eyes. Doesn't own a TV, streams

podcasts on weekends. Then a warm bath,

calcium pills, dictionary work. Lists of winged

animals & migratory patterns, a half-opened hymnal

next to the toothpaste. Once visited a jailhouse,

returned home with poems about bees.

Views her talent, simply, as a lesser Keats.

Working on self-image, positive reinforcement,

expanding wardrobe to reveal true personality.

If only solitude were reproducible!

If only an intricate hair-pinning regimen

equaled vigilance to the mind. A poem can go

one of many ways, like my niece plays dress-up:

bohemian/hippie/New Wave/preppy/

saint/post-punk/Gladys Knight & the Pips/

David Foster Wallace. I suffer difficulties

regarding mode—both speech & transportation.

The kitchen fan whirrs like a UFO:

I feel its blades, metallic, gaping.

In her recurring dream of a car underwater,

there's no charger in sight, but the landscape

roams blue for miles. Nerves wrapped

like a box set, bobbing with selfness;

semi-colon in a comma crowd.

Supermarket as projection of how choice

crushes, unread messages in the inbox, chronic

summer sales: thinks she'd like a new dress

but can't stomach fitting rooms.

Prefers to be online.

Today feels more afflicted, due to weather.

I recorded my eating—hard cheese,

fragments of bread & the never-getting-full.

Planted bulbs in the garden, wrote a poem

about a violet bird. Loneliness is bearable

in daylight, on cramped checkout lines,

but night unveils longing at its acutest:

a cusp of moon through the window,

cars honking, too many at once to separate

so why try. A hunger with the drawers bare.

Like the sun, death hovers, a disk in air.

There's no fear but a nagging itch to know.

Small griefs still sting—disappearance

of family dog at age six, distant mother,

that pulsing eye, loss of childhood, etc.

When friends hopped trains to California,

she stayed home, hell-bent, then glimpsed

their photos, a gaggle of girls hamming it up

in the Haight. Avoidance as means of coping.

Learned habits. Must expand toolbox.

The body is another beast entirely.

At the gym the same women riding the same

machines & ride really does seem to be the right

word here—an erotic victory! How defeating

the machines & thus the body mirrors sex.

Self-sabotage sinks its teeth in.

Snow solves the problem of arrival.

Besides, how to say the thought of sex

feels like a thorn in the gut but also a hole?

The worst kind of uncovering.

What to wear to dinner & what to eat,

how to draw another in, should crimson

be changed to red & does the change matter—

the same thoughts scramble on a loop.

The strands never straighten or offer answers.

In her best dream, has a simple shirt

& someone to walk the strobe-lit river with,

who doesn't mind an unmade face.

Rigid adherence to track changes

optional. Severe intelligence a must

& gables upon gables of idiomatic speech,

who tells me I can be a planet / all petals

turn blue in the right kind of dark.

Or I become industrious: what a difference

a good house-cleaning makes!

The countertops, rose tub & hardwood

possess perfect clarity, like the emptiness

of a frozen field at dusk. A dense silver

overrun with weeds. I stand at the eastern edge.

Bend to pluck one up.

I WANT TO BE SINCERE NOW

My worst nightmare is talking
on the phone for hours, my best
a Staten Island Ferry ride
or the time I joined an equestrian team,
jumping over fences, the ribboning meadow.
I wasn't scared though I've never
touched a horse in this life.
In this life I want one microwaveable
meal, clear answer on a test,
a cloud chamber where I can listen
to the wind distort. My back
will be hooked to tubes charting
my progress as a human. I sleep stacked
among my books. How am I doing?

ON TURNING THIRTY

No one microwaves leftovers, we order in.
I haven't prayed since 1996.
In temple the cantor was always tuning her guitar
& the metal folding chairs squeaked.
Is hypnosis dead?
I feel about as sexual as a frying pan.
At this age Sylvia had sheaves of poems,
two kids &—
my aura drips like a sieve.
According to the internet, the small ache
in our chest derives from artificial sweeteners,
anxiety, too much aptitude.
Better that than bad genes or apathy.
I wish I thought I'd be married by now.

BLUE GLACIERS

Your parents go on vacation
& ask you to housesit.
They have two cats,
which were your cats
when you were younger,
so you stay to feed them
& make turkey sandwiches,
put out the recycling, get the mail.
The cats wander around
all day & only go outside
on sunny afternoons
& you wonder if they are cold
or hungry but realize
they are just lonely,
looking for a warm body
to lie next to. Since you have
often felt this way,
you let them stay with you
during *Breaking Bad*
& at night you can't sleep because
they keep trying to curl
themselves on top of your feet.
In your parents' house are paintings
your grandfather made
& photographs & sculptures
from countries they've visited.
In your apartment are similar

paintings & photographs
& hardcover books you share.
You are at an age where it is
a reality that your parents will
in your near-enough future
die & that thought swells
in your chest like a large boat
in a much larger ocean.
When you sit on your porch,
you imagine the family
who will one day live there,
how in school their children
will learn the routes of explorers,
which queens they served
& goods they traded for.
You water your mother's plants,
wash the cans of cat food
& sleep in your bed beneath
class pictures from middle school,
when the world was just
as rigged, but maybe you felt
hopeful, like a baseball field's
bright foul lines before a game.
Sometimes you don't know
how you made it this far
since you can barely do things
like pack boxes to ship
across the country

or use a stove in any real capacity.
You worry you won't be someone
good enough to marry.
At night, you watch the NewsHour special
on blue glaciers in the Arctic,
then find an extra blanket
to sleep with, a cream-colored wool.
In the morning you wake
to scratches at your door
& it's the cats who insist it's time,
it's time now to get up
& go outside.

SUPPORTING ROLE

I make a halo with my hands.
Loyal friend who provides
pithy, essential wisdom.

I help the main character
reach her potential, as a woman
secure in relationships.

All scenery is transitional.
Pink clouds zap across the sky,
a tree replete with branches,

night opening into day. Hello there,
(me) at the edge of the frame—
please give separating

your recyclables a try.
A baby wails in a crib off-screen.
No world is complete. No

snow in this one, just a moon
that drops behind buildings
& laptop glow like a grail.

Now cut to me in the dark
with no real thoughts, forgetting
to floss. I have never flossed.

2.

LIVES OF THE TWENTY-FIRST-CENTURY FEMALE POETS

after Katha Pollitt

They grew up mostly inside their heads.
A little neurotic, adored by their fathers,

trying to hide or stand out in vintage.
Smoked their first cigarettes on escalators

at the mall or in the woods, planetary,
with an older cousin. One read Millay

by flashlight, one was a ranked pianist,
another only a suitcase & broken zipper

in a bus depot. Mothers are acute migraines
& god-like. They overbear or leave early.

Some, now mothers themselves, use the
same pecan pie recipe, some are childless.

To us, they're gigantics of therapy-talk &
botched abortions, brainwaves caught over

open flame, like a hot-plate of ambivalence.
Spot on our blackest tie. Their morning selves

made lists. Nights, they stuck the Post-its
to blades of grass, gathered the neon blooms.

SOMETIMES, GENDER

Girls are quick to turn sour
like milk or lemons. Boys grow antlers.
At recess in the cold, I scuffed the edges
of both circles, played team sports
& the piano. Sometimes gender
needs a new winter coat, or a blowtorch
& homemade mix-tape. We ate Twizzlers
at *Titanic*, taped Leo to our doors.
I watched the wallpaper peel, figured
action was overrated. In order of importance
I saved my day-glo diary & Latin books,
while boy bands bloomed like anthills
on my mother's lawn. I wanted to be
popular, then smart, then someone's
favorite, instead got a laptop & back-page
editorial in the yearbook. I wrote *Action*
is impractical if the war is faceless.
I had a crush on every girl who smoked
in the gymnasium basement. At night
every star looked like a pearl, but close up
each one was faithless, close up my body
ruthless. I cried when my best friend
got a real boyfriend, the water polo captain.
Sex was temporary, tenuous. Our tenth-
grade history teacher—we called him Heath—
was born Heather. We didn't know
until later. Imperceptible the difference
between phenotype & Photoshop, pronouns
& antecedents, my body, its fixed uses.

WHAT IT WAS LIKE, BEING A GIRL

bleached my best shirt out
in winter stood bone still

as if a gray sky were good as new
membrane posing as shell

why I did everything backward
iced a cake before it burned

lies I never learned to tell
the girls with wool sweaters

& space for their desires
sliced into the snow

I trailed the one I wanted
to the art room's alcove

some boy said shut up & hurry
that door—you're letting in the cold

I bought an electric toothbrush
because the dentist said I wasn't thorough enough
& wants to see me in two months.
The therapist prophesied a near-recovery,
predicted love would come eventually.
When the conductor asked for my ticket
the subtext was he'd been working
ten hours straight & could use a smoke break,
but I had nothing to offer.

Now at night, I brush & brush to the whir
of the small machine, screen my calls,
put lettuce on tomorrow's sandwich.
I imagine I'm being interviewed
on a leather couch on a talk show set
& when I tell a story about middle school
dances, everyone laughs. Outside, two teenagers
argue over video game graphics. On TV,
the finalists sing for their lives.

SELF-PORTRAIT AS PEGGY OLSON FROM *MAD MEN*

1.

We watch them watch us
patent our lips

red—

coral reef, grenadine,
Mars afterglow.

It's a long way from Bay Ridge,

where I wasn't
valedictorian

but could hold my breath
longest of any girl.

2.

Real girls have roommates.

They live together
above Laundromats,

prefer contacts, at the diner
order cottage cheese

with a side of neon peaches.

How do they manage
a smoky eye in any weather

or convince a man
there's always more

tomorrow, the day after?

I'm all ears & all
thumbs, it's all Greek to me,

but I'm a quick study.
I color-code my notes.

3.

I want you
like a can of Heinz beans
wants a ballpark frank,

how light hits a Chevy
in glossy print, with just
a hint of red.

When the jet wing
slices a cloud, all air escapes
my lungs

& your hand's at my throat
again in bed in my one
good dream.

I don't know how to unloosen.
After a few drinks,
I say the opposite

of what I mean,
a vagueness when I can't
feel my freedom.

In night's flesh
I make myself a rope,
keep what I hold.

4.

after Lily Brown

Unhooked him, flunked trig,
rebooted. Tracked footprints

onto the carpet. Learned Latin,
got hung up in semantic webs

& drenched at dusk. Went
postal. Voted, subdued the hoi

polloi, manned a dim cellar.
Kept some dignity. What's left

but a theoretical me? Recited
a canto, flipped pancakes, wore

heels. Made sure nails dried.
Worked sick. Won the office pool.

5.

I've tried to be a man.

It doesn't work & anyway
I don't know I want to.

I see how they make
themselves go home at night,

eyes light—blank as glass.

I've strained to be impersonal,
smile through my teeth.

I don't like cigarettes
& I work weekends

just because. Come over.
I know it's late. Yes, I need

you, I always do.

MARIE HOWE'S LOVE POEM FOR THE GIRLS SHE KISSED IN SEVENTH GRADE DOESN'T RING TRUE TO MY EXPERIENCE

It wasn't hymn-like or complicit.
There was no plush carpet,

no *desirous thrill*. Can I say I felt
like an island? Is that old-fashioned?

January & I dreamed myself thin
or glue-gunned to someone else's

skin & thighs. There were two types
of girls: either you loved Kurt Cobain

or horses. I wanted both, badly, but
without language. No one is the boy

& gets away with it. Or I'd make
myself stand in a locker-room stall,

still in school clothes where my eyes
wouldn't wander. It was winter.

The trees tried to shake their frost.
I lay awake at night waiting for anything.

LENA DUNHAM'S *GIRLS*

Please fuck me—forward, backward
or upside down. I'll wear fishnets

& a hoodie, you'll make a joke about
Lexapro & my three extra pounds.

Then to the laser party with ankle
bracelets & pills no one's heard of &

at dinner with my parents I'll develop
vertigo. I'll go home early, eat vanilla

fro yo & hot dogs, check Facebook, text
the gynecologist. This is what it's like

to be us right now—we're craning
our necks downward for a closer view.

Your acoustic mash-up of my memoir
just went viral & see how the skyline

looks so real? That's because it is. We
shoot on location. We're as it as it gets.

RIDING AN OVERNIGHT TRAIN

a field like water
intimations   of woodlands

road signs glint
O delicate   compulsory work

my body   a slope
I fall back   stand very still

it is the way sometimes
to be quiet   & complicit

to follow a note   to its completion
it is the way sometimes

blue   stars in the distance
get their reverb

the night loosens   breaks into waves
I climb a tree

prepare for the dark
to set in   a bell rings

like a shot   the sky
begs to erupt

THE OFF-SEASON

I wanted to wake up in another town
where the snow would skim me,
          just barely. Branches cracked in the woods
    behind my house,
        shadows bent to the shape of a mother.
           In my fatalist's memory

it's perpetual winter, like walking into wind.
    The days shortened
         & shortened
            on a slack leash.

Because this is modern suburbia, I had a graphing calculator
         & copy of *A Separate Peace*, parents
    shuttling me to basketball practice & piano,

    a friend who didn't invite me to her ice-skating party
        at the indoor rink the next zip code over—

    in these ways I was every girl
  who wished for a future
    where she could turn her body
           off like a light switch,
           small switchblade,
           closed zipper.

*

On TV in 1995, Angela Chase was inhabiting flannel,
       trying to decide whether to sleep with Jordan Catalano
          & Ricky Vasquez was gay & homeless

   & not blending in.

I was busy talking back to teachers, who gave me detention.
I wouldn't change
         in the locker room
                with the other girls.

After everyone left, I could be alone in my body—
      as the radiator clanked too loudly,
         the brick walls & metal lockers
                without locks
                   closed in—

        but that scared me too, like wanting to look
at their flat stomachs & their lacrosse sticks
& their field hockey sticks & their blond ponytails
     & their hair ribbons on game days
              so I turned away.

At night I used a ruler by desk lamp
       to divide my paper into columns,
            to isolate the variable

& if *girls* was the variable, it was impossible to be their friend—
                    I must have seemed like some
          mix of class clown,

                              lap dog & foreign
                                   exchange student

like the time I wrote an essay
          defining the word "perfect"
          as Natalie Phillips, the most popular girl in school—

          (What possibly could it have said? That she brushed
          her blond hair, cleaned her retainer,
          had a hockey-player boyfriend?)

& handed it in to my teacher, a retired jock,
who took me aside & told me

I should stop trying to be friends with girls like Natalie
& stick to being friends with the two girls in my class who were

like me
                    which is to say *boyish*,
                    which is to say *weird*,
                    which is to say *ugly*,

& for all these things the principal set up a meeting
with my parents & told them I should see a therapist.

*

I thrashed in my bed when my parents suggested it.

*

In the museums I saw the great paintings,
                                                    face of a windmill,
                                        face of regret.

Vermeer's girls & Sargent's girls & Hopper's girls
all looked the same to me: pallid, disaffected,
                                    resigned to a life without desires.

At the end of our driveway, my father put up a hoop,
                & weekend mornings, bouncing a flat ball,
                            I'd dare myself to stare into the sun,

hoping that if I could outlast the glare, I might learn some secret
                        I could keep, like a bookmark, tucked away

different from the one I already had
& couldn't say out loud,
                    a way to meet the world
                                        head-on, face the narrow
                                                    brightness—

*

In 1997 Ellen came out on the cover of *Time*.
I saw it in Borders with my mom
while researching the Reconstruction.

      It was like falling down a well, literally.
            Or clinging to rocks against a strong current
                  unable to let the feeling go—
                        that landscape of inwardness.

Instead, I became invisible,
      a habit worth forming as I was growing
            uncontained—
& knew who I was
            wouldn't fit—

I wore my father's clothes
            until I understood not to,
anyone who looked like me made me panic—

In spring, as coach of my softball team he drove us all home
one Sunday, past the library, past McDonalds,
      when suddenly from the backseat

                  the loudest, skinniest girl with a bad attitude
                      glared at me & blurted out
                 (I don't think there was any other context)

Are you gay?

I had no idea what to say—
the words rose in the air,
        that space girls make
                to prick each other—

so I said *No!*

& the other girls laughed
& I thought about how in my uniform I looked just like them
so how could they know?

*

In Ovid, girls are always turning
into trees, stiff in their roots
like a ruffled collar.

I used to think either way a girl can't win—she's seen
& it ends in tragedy or she's unseen,
which is worse.

42

Apollo hovers in Daphne's exclusive air,
tries to get on top of her, sticky inside her, so she can never get
him out—

(He's at her shoulders now; she feels his breath upon the hair
that streams down her neck)

but I think it matters that in Daphne's story
it's she & not the god who gets
the last, best
word.

(As soon as she is finished with her prayer,
a heavy numbness grips her limbs;
thin bark is changed

to leaves, her arms
to boughs, the girl's head vanishes,
becomes a crown.)

Also, it turns out she liked being a tree.

*

Like an anthropologist,
I studied girls
who lived in mesh shorts
& hooded sweatshirts,
who played sports
or didn't wear makeup,
to see how they carried their bodies,
to see if they talked to boys,
went with them to the woods—
or else, like me, stayed
closed, an off-season motel.

I never found the answers,
          not in school with the coked-up
          anorexic girls

          or the bohemian artists
                    or the football players
          or the smart stoners
                    who claimed Keats & Pynchon both.

I found an article about Melissa Etheridge
who said she came out at seventeen & I thought,

Well, I have two more years for this feeling to pass
          before it never will.

*

As a lyric: a worm had sewn itself into my skin
& I was the worm.

*

As a narrative: there were weekend parties
        at someone's parents' house, team huddles,

shacks in the woods
where kids went to have sex

        & I was there but absent for all of it,
                covered under leaves like the dead bird.

*

As rhetoric: owned one jacket to outlast the winter,
        ran one mile
                around the indoor track,
wrote one list of Latin verbs.

*

As metaphor: late afternoons I practiced layups
　　　in dull light, cramming the air into my lungs,
　　　　　　　where there was more space to move.

3.

REPRISE

This is a new section, signaling time has passed. So I get older,
grow up, feel mostly the same.

There is a you sometimes, but typically just an I.
        The you comes in & out of focus,
                like looking into the sun then looking away,
                        a dream that recurs
                    as if to prove its existence.

Sometimes I write the you into my current body,
        the bookstore reading or the hospital
                the night I cut my foot open,
a text that says come over this late
& this is still the dream talking,
                        the sutures, the lukewarm bath,
                            three voicemails,
the changing leaves, the birds' black
                        wings on the window ledge.

Is that you, walking across a field in snow,
        in Alphabet City, in the photo with the band t-shirt,
                dating an athlete, then a femme girl,
            then a crazy European?

Maybe I'm there too, in the field in the snow
            or waking early to run on a broken treadmill,

& we must have driven all of Vermont's back roads
        in your beat-up Civic

(one summer you dove into the lake, the stars nicked you,
we glowed faintly)

                    until it was not-enough love, not-enough
        air & you didn't want me
                & I kept standing next to the unfrozen river.

In the end you got what you wanted:
        I heard your boyfriend works in sales, roots for the Patriots

            & I wonder if this is even a story worth telling
    because it's not dangerous, just a little sad

            like a kid's best stone that won't skip,
        or trying to smoke a cigarette
                under water. It's the way,
                    only later,

        love can stand outside
                        itself, guileless,

                    cold.

THE AGGRESSIVENESS OF SEX CRUSHES ME

rain starts then stalls

every one of my off-brand desires

the girls at the bar

in sleeveless denim & Bauhaus haircuts

like experiments for a new gender

would I recognize you now

that you date men

& live in a city we never liked

maybe I'll fall asleep to a stranger

cutting imaginary hair

& breathing into a camera

These layers really flatter your face

I'm still looking for a door

some small sky to sink into

WHEN I CAN'T FALL ASLEEP, SOMETIMES I WANDER AROUND DUANE READE

on display tonight

all the translucent emergencies:

someone reciting wedding vows

past midnight

the last full carton of half-priced milk

an infinity of appetites

to be absolved or fossilized

in the alternating silence

& lowlight hum of aisle twelve

a baby yawns

cascade of snow

our entire history spins

on this myth of what we own

its analog glow

REALITY SHOW

In this episode a famous poet comes to speak.
She's on speed, possibly
suicidal but has perfectly toned arms,
so I'm not sure whether to pity or envy her.
I try to starve myself
by eating three handfuls of pita chips.
I run on the treadmill then walk.
I wipe my sweat.
In montage I mourn the boy killed by his classmate
for liking to wear heels & makeup,
also the jury's devastating hearts
that go out to the shooter
because twenty-one years is a lot of time
like the time it takes to get over middle school.
A girl once told me I'd be more attractive
if I acted butch—I don't even know what that means
practically speaking, the voice-over
as I swim backstroke in the public pool
& pluck hairs from my face like an Olympian.

IMPERFECT SYSTEM

1.

night is an imperfect system

of expectation

a human-fed wind

I don't own gloves or a purse

or any useful thing

I list novels I've skimmed

not even good ones

we check our mirrored reflections

your voice skips

in my peripheral vision

too late for sex

itself a form of flight

still you leave a partial print

& symptoms

2.

tonight it rains so hard

umbrellas skid across the streets

like tumbleweed

across a windblown plain

someone somewhere

is singing a hip-hop song

neon glistens

next to the subway

we're soaked & amplified

with newness

I try to zip up your jacket

but the zipper sticks

your face abstract

your hair so long & dark

3.

finally I am not a hologram

my fingers curl & uncurl

we perpetually regret New

Jersey & the Internet

I've tossed my best t-shirt

the wine all my Latin

my fear packed like a grove

of trees in fog my desire

is also the grove but dark

like a chestnut on your

tongue my mouth a flood-

light two red birds your

hands at my waist go lower so

this is what a body is for

4.

what I love does not make me ashamed

that which you want me

to do to you I do

also other things that require

your breath on my breath

your skin on my breath

at the winter beach

there are rolled cigarettes

a girl with headphones

& I am becoming certain

waves crest & fall in any season

as long as gravity persists

we speak with our own inflections

we're infectious

5.

when you leave

I swallow my concavity

I'm trying not to

take things personally

watch me arrange

the salt shakers perfectly

I've been practicing

my laugh track & how to run

like a corporation

on the empty boardwalk

even the birds expect

an ending everyone knows

but you like the future best

its cursive legs

AFTER THE FLOOD

When the rains came, I was busy baking bread,
harnessing the think tank, watching the latest
dance craze sweep the nation while folding your
pajamas. Luckily, we had a spare wooden boat
in the corner of the garage near the paint cans
& snow shovels so we made our escape
via the cul-de-sac. Now, twenty days after leaving
our small house with the partial view of the pond,
we're floating by discarded sneakers, kids
with antlers, a treetop where soda bottles once nested
& I have the urge to style your hair some new
way, but it's matted down & feels like agriculture.
To pass the time we're singing TV sitcom themes
& playing Guess What Chain This Part Of The Ocean
Used To Be—*Walmart, Dunkin' Donuts, Williams Sonoma.*
In Twenty Questions, I am a handmade Christmas
ornament, you are Hulk Hogan's trimmed mustache.
Me: the oatmeal you were forced to eat at the Mother
Goose Nursery School. You: the phantom braces
you swear I wore as a teenager. Me: Wichita, Kansas.
You: the broken button on the coffee machine.
In the distance, radishes & bits of licorice congeal
in the scenery like aspic. Chicken wire & cell phones
are poking out from beneath the thunderstorms.
When we wake to radio reports that state colleges
have dissolved to reservoirs, you will be the alphabet

kids learn to recite under water. But for now
I'm wrapping your shoelaces around my fingertips
& you're trying to get some sleep. Faint lights flicker.
We're the groundhog's early shadow.

ME AT THE END

Like the familiar gestures

we rehearsed, a cup

half-filled with liquid.

We of the great escapes

to the outer boroughs

for borscht. It happened

until it stopped. Here,

take my self-awareness

& self-starter mentality—

I prefer to follow. Dangle

me at the end of any line.

In the moon-dark, invisible,

I'll be your shadow.

You'll barely know I exist.

A FEW THINGS I WOULD LIKE

full knowledge of the lives of saints

another set of keys

a long sleep where there is another you

in a distant room

radio hits I haven't heard in years

a window seat on the local train

fields & fields

for all my cavities to be removed

prescriptions filled

the hiss & crackle

of oil in a pan

fresh loaves of bread

for the crusts to flake onto our shirts

for us to brush them off

DRIVING THROUGH VERMONT AT DUSK

In towns that could be anywhere
in America, you are exactly

yourself, joined to a flawed body,
sanded & smoothed, a shelf

without varnish. When the last light
shreds the sky, you'll lie awake

alone or with someone, below stars,
their indistinct edges. Believe in all of it,

that closer distance, & the wind
still as an understudy, ready to go on.

4.

FOREIGNNESS BREEDS THAT SHARED LANGUAGE, THE BRAIN IN TRANSLATION (DEAR ELIZABETH BISHOP)

1.

It took me awhile
to warm up to you.
Your poems felt cool

to my wobbly
sophomoric eye,
meticulous, controlled,

lacking the accessible
confessional self
I'd grown used to:

where was the bleeding
heart? When I got older,
I read more, parsed

the moment *Write it!*
breaks through,
went to Greece, then Peru

to dodge the world
until it found me
recording the colors

of houses along the coast
& names of fruits
I couldn't pronounce.

On top of Machu Picchu
with an iPod & Gatorade,
I snapped pictures

of tourists' ubiquitous
cargo vests; a red flower
peeked from under a rock.

I think it's true, all travelers
want to be a window
to experience,

letting light & sound
pass through us,
or else we stay shut.

2.

How did you manage
without a mother?

Did you grow up faster
or did it take longer

to learn to be a girl?
In Newfoundland

for the summer, you
& your college friends

tote heavy sweaters,
magazines & cigarettes

along the beach, sneak
beers onto the bluffs.

I picture you quoting
Shakespeare off the cuff,

gossiping about a handsome
senior, pining for a dress

you can't afford but
will likely buy anyway.

At a graduation party
from boarding school

in Connecticut, I get drunk
for the first time & fall

asleep in a coat closet,
between someone's

mother's furs. Empty
bottles sprout like strange,

translucent foliage.
Night goes on without me.

3.

Elizabeth, you could get married now
if you wanted to. In fact, there's a new

movie about you & Lota living together
in Brazil called *Reaching for the Moon*—

can you think of a worse title? It feels
faraway, like an impressionist painting.

In the trailer, you're repressed, buttoned
up & in your poems sometimes too.

But lately I've been reading your letters,
filled with all kinds of humor & obscenities!

In one of my favorites, you've just won
the Pulitzer & describe an interview

your aunt gave to the Worcester paper:
With true family ambivalence she announced

I would have made a great piano player
(I don't believe she ever heard me play

the piano once) & that "lots & lots of people
don't like her poetry, of course!"

Aunt Florence could be my grandmother,
who, when my father published his first book,

maintained his best work was an essay
about the Vikings he'd written at age ten—

she'd helped him edit it. In an earlier letter,
you have just taken a corner apartment

in Greenwich Village, a fixer-upper,
& stand by impishly while the electrician

fishes through your closet for a phone line.
It's comforting to know you held

the same good-natured uncertainty as most
of us moving to New York after college.

(My first apartment in the Bronx, last stop
on the 6 train, featured water bugs & no heat.

The second, we were sure, belonged to
the mafia—our landlady was missing a finger

she tried to wag at us, offered almond biscotti
& only accepted cash, up-front & in-person.)

Now I'm trying to reconcile all the you's—
the poetry-you & the letter-you & the bad-

film-you—none of which, I guess,
is the you-you, though all are parts of you.

4.

I try to put sex in a poem.
I can only get it into the title.

My teacher says, *I like this*
but where's the sex? The poem doesn't really

deliver
& she's right, though I feel a little vulgar

putting sex in,
not that I'm having any,

so a little disingenuous too,
now that *cock* & *slit* & *blowjob*

appear in every other line
of every other online poem

as if to prove we're doing it
in all ways as standard as breathing

& all the fabulous
non-standard ways too—

I prefer the hair-washing intimacy
you intimate:

close as two pages
in a book . . .

A little progress:
last month, I went to a reading

at a sex shop! Practiced
my nonchalance as the liquids & leathers,

the thick-thin-round-sharp-red-black-
glass-silicon-cinnamon-flavored-king-size-

rainbow-sprinkled-holed-strapped-
snapped-lipped-flapped-

apparatuses
gleamed—

& not to backpedal,
but *must* a poetry reading take place at a sex shop?

Then again, why not
& why not a gutter, parking lot, bathtub

or the Sahara,
for that matter?

The first poet explained
how when she moved to New York five years ago

she picked Park Slope
because she wanted a girlfriend

then proceeded to read a long poem
about sex with a series of men,

& I admired her flexibility, fluidity, un-apology
(& she was very attractive)

(& the next poet said, *That was the saddest
poem I've ever heard*)

(& a young poet I've only seen online
wouldn't get off his phone the whole time)

but I'm exhausted too,
because every part of us

seems about as solid as water—
nothing holds.

5.

Did they hold—
the Key West trinkets
you enclosed for Marianne?

A leaf, beans, a stingray's
stinger, so she could feel
Florida from her cramped

apartment in Brooklyn?
Your letters are like music
boxes stuffed with junk,

the bits of life we witness
or turn over: the *ancient*
& decaying shells of oysters

shared by three gum-chewing boys
on the steamer from Europe
alongside cages & cages of owls

who eat hearts. Elizabeth,
have you seen Matisse's cut-outs?
They're at the MoMA now;

his process of pinning
the gouache shapes
cut & recut with scissors

on canvas then rearranging them
sounds like the closest thing
to poetry I've found in art.

(Never mind his assistants
were all overworked young women.)
In my favorite mural

a parakeet perches in one corner,
a mermaid in the other
between leaves & pomegranates—

a forest or garden—
like the oranges & pinks
of Key West summers.

The notes said Matisse
identified with the parakeet:
it was how he became himself

in his art. Why the parakeet
floating in air & also
who is the mermaid

dropped into the garden,
neither blue nude nor diver?
What does a mermaid do in a garden?

What do you identify with
in your work: are you the weed
or lost keys or the disaster?

The icebergs, fire balloons
or the interior? Does it matter?
Are we the art itself,

the only place we can escape
or become who we really are?
I'm sure I've always only been the *I*.

6.

after Frank O'Hara

Elizabeth, what do you want to know
about now? Some poets are still alive

& writing to stay that way despite
half-hearted gun laws & a lack

of vacation days or rain in California.
We have pocket-sized machines

that connect us from room to room,
so we can see another's face

on a screen in time, but somehow
the effect falls flat & flattens us,

like staring at yourself in a mirror.
Black boys are still being killed

in flocks—if only they were migrating
toward warmer weather—

but yesterday my student Gabriel
shared with us how his neighbors say

he has the hands of a doctor
(though secretly he wants to be a writer)

& that once a teacher told him, *Gabriel,*
someday I'm going to see you

on the news—& I couldn't help but hear
two meanings in that prophecy,

while the class held still for a breath
& he didn't recognize the irony,

a kind of blessing, but said he felt so
good about himself that day the teacher

had confidence in him it almost
brought me & everyone to tears, too.

7.

Most days I can't decide whether flaunting our freedom makes us more or less free, like when my college's alumni magazine runs a cover story about gay couples raising children (title: "Modern Families") & Rich Thompson '93, only ten years older than me, who lives less than thirty miles from me, feels moved to respond: *I would like to express my dismay at this magazine's promotion of homosexual lifestyle & choice. I am fully aware that a portion of the United States has accepted non-traditional lifestyles & values. However, as a Christian with a traditional family, I feel it is neither appropriate nor in the interest of our alma mater.* I wish the magazine hadn't printed the original article to begin with, then feel guilty for wishing it.

8.

When I find you next, in a letter
to Miss Moore, you & Louise

have just observed two swans
sitting on their eggs, turning them

every half hour, exactly. We went
to watch them do it—with their feet—

& it is the nicest thing afterward
to see the mother swan stretch

her neck around so as to confirm
all the eggs are underneath...

I wonder how long you must have
stayed to know the swans turn

every half hour, exactly—today,
no one I know could bear to *be*

for more than a few seconds, until
the next bright text comes through,

heaped on a thread. Last week
in Connecticut I walked the beach

at dusk—it's November & cool,
skeletons of boats clanked in the wind,

their masts all wire & no sails.
Kayaks, single-hued, were stacked

for the off-season. (Actually, I've never
seen those kayaks used by anyone,

even in summer.) In the distance
grew the great gray silhouette of Manhattan,

abstract Sound, bruise-colored hills,
yellowing reeds. A heron tiptoed

on the sand, then dipped his head.
I was the only one to see him do it.

What if these small solitudes,
a thought in a journal or partial line

of a poem, a memory from middle school,
were to nick our shared consciousness

like a gasp of breath or loose change—
do we feel another's silence in us?

Back in Manhattan, the pedestrians
walk briskly under streetlights, the taxis

don't stop for anyone, a crosstown bus
lets down its ramp, but perhaps somewhere

you & others may know my evening
of the heron, the way your letters,

those personal correspondences,
now make a kind of public archive,

so that when you write to Frani Blough,
following a digression about jazz,

I haven't spoken to anyone all day
& all my random forces are coming out,

you have of course been speaking
to us, this late & this early, the whole time.

NOTES

"I Want To Be Sincere Now": Lines from the poem are indebted to Jennifer B. Thoreson's "Medic" series & Amanda Friberg's "still lives #3."

"Lives of the Twenty-First Century Female Poets": The title & poem refer to Katha Pollitt's poem "Lives of the Nineteenth-Century Poetesses." The final line is inspired by Thomas Jackson's "Emergent Behavior" series. The poem is for my teachers at NYU.

"What It Was Like, Being A Girl": The title is borrowed from Deborah Eisenberg's story "What It Was Like, Seeing Chris."

"Self-Portrait as Peggy Olson from *Mad Men*": In section 1, the opening lines borrow from Miranda Field's poem "The Parties." Section 4 is, in parts, a sound translation of Lily Brown's poem "Mapped Music."

"The Off-Season": Italicized lines come from Book I of Ovid's *Metamorphoses* translated by Allen Mandelbaum.

"Driving Through Vermont at Dusk" is for Cleopatra Mathis.

"Foreignness Breeds That Shared Language, the Brain in Translation (Dear Elizabeth Bishop)": Some of the italicized lines come from Elizabeth Bishop's poems & letters, the latter with slight revisions for sound.

ACKNOWLEDGMENTS

Thank you to the editors of the following journals, in which versions of these poems first appeared:

Bodega, Boston Review, CutBank, DIAGRAM, The Literary Review, No, Dear, PHANTOM, Sixth Finch, & *Tin House.*

I would like to express my sincerest thanks to my teachers, past & present, for being so generous with their time & for their encouragement; my friends for all their help with poems & life; Martha, Ryan & Four Way Books for this opportunity; & my family, who mean everything to me.

Jen Levitt received her MFA from NYU. Her poems have appeared in *Boston Review*, *DIAGRAM*, *Sixth Finch*, *Tin House* and elsewhere. She lives in New York City and teaches high school students.

MN
NW

Publication of this book was made possible by grants and donations.
We are also grateful to those individuals who participated in our
2015 Build a Book Program. They are:

Jan Bender-Zanoni, Betsy Bonner, Deirdre Brill, Carla & Stephen Carlson,
Liza Charlesworth, Catherine Degraw & Michael Connor, Greg Egan,
Martha Webster & Robert Fuentes, Anthony Guetti, Hermann Hesse,
Deming Holleran, Joy Jones, Katie Childs & Josh Kalscheur, Michelle King,
David Lee, Howard Levy, Jillian Lewis, Juliana Lewis, Owen Lewis,
Alice St. Claire Long & David Long, Catherine McArthur, Nathan McClain,
Carolyn Murdoch, Tracey Orick, Kathleen Ossip, Eileen Pollack, Barbara
Preminger, Vinode Ramgopal, Roni Schotter, Soraya Shalforoosh,
Marjorie & Lew Tesser, David Tze, Abby Wender, and Leah Nanako Winkler.